ONLY WATER BETWEEN: A FAMILY STORY OF THE GREAT WAR

ONLY WATER BETWEEN: A FAMILY STORY OF THE GREAT WAR

Angela Clare

Also published by Royal Armouries

Arms and Armour of the First World War (2017)

Saving Lives: Sir Arthur Conan Doyle and the Campaign for Body Armour, 1914–18 (2017)

Stumbling Towards Victory: The Final Year of the Great War (2018)

Archduke Franz Ferdinand and the Era of Assassination (2018)

Published by Royal Armouries Museum, Armouries Drive, Leeds LS10 1LT, United Kingdom

www.royalarmouries.org

ISBN 978 1 91301 303 5 (print)
ISBN 978 1 91301 304 2 (epub)

Typesetting by Newgen Publishing UK
Printed by 4edge

10 9 8 7 6 5 4 3 2 1

A CIP record for this book is available from the British Library

'My love story has been equal to anyone in the world
and leaves nothing to be desired'

– Jack Adam to Gert Adam, 4 February 1918

'It's only water between'

– Jack Adam to Gert Adam, 15 March 1918

1 Photograph of Jack and Gert Adam. © Royal Armouries. ADAM A5/4.

CONTENTS

ILLUSTRATIONS

All images courtesy of the Trustees of the Royal Armouries.

PREFACE

Taken from a family archive held at the Royal Armouries Museum in Leeds, this book tells the story of Jack and Gert Adam and their three young children during the First World War. *Only Water Between* serves as a moving reminder of the impact of the Great War on the lives of so many million individuals and families throughout the world.

The letters written by Jack and Gert Adam reveal the strength of the couple and their three children, separated by the demands of the war. In 1918, Jack is deployed to serve his country in France and does not make it home again. This volume contains extracts and images of archival letters, photos and related documents telling this family's experience of the war through separation. It describes the war years, when there was 'only water between' them, together with the impact of soldiers who were missing in action, and the remarkable story of their children. The archive has its own unique story of an accidental loss, discovery and reunion decades after the war ended.

As war has continued to mark the twentieth and twenty-first centuries, this family's account is as relevant as ever. Their story emulates the experiences and feelings of so many people who have experienced separation through the demands of warfare and the dramatic upheaval of their normal lives, which may never again return to their former contentment.

ACKNOWLEDGEMENTS

This book is edited by Angela Clare, who worked for the Royal Armouries for several years and has shared Jack and Gert Adam's story through theatre, talks and in print. Angela played the role of Gert in the play *Only Water Between* at the Royal Armouries and at the Edinburgh Fringe in August 2009. She continues to work in museums, sharing historical collections, archives and stories with audiences through a variety of media.[1]

Thanks are due primarily to Philip Abbott at the Royal Armouries for initially acquiring the collection and seeing its potential as a relatable story to share the impact of the First World War on individuals, and his encouragement for the production, talks and this publication. Thanks also to Peter Spafford who initially researched the collection and created the play 'Only Water Between', and the actors who have performed it over the years. Also, to the descendants of Jack and Gert who not only supported the play but also donated further collections and kindly shared their family story with us.

The Adam archive and collection items are held by the Royal Armouries in Leeds.

1 An abridged version of this story with a focus on Gert Adam appeared as A. Clare, 'A personal account of the Home Front', in M. Andrews and J. Lomas (eds.), *The Home Front in Britain: Images, Myths and Forgotten Experiences since 1914* (London, 2014: Palgrave Macmillan), 21–38.

INTRODUCTION

Rather than statistics of numbers killed, families divided, women widowed, and children left fatherless during the First World War, it is reading an individual's letters that connect us most viscerally to countless experiences of separation and grief at that time. These personal memories also add to the diversity of experiences from this period as we look back over the century since the end of the war in 1918.[1]

At the heart of the war, it was not tactics but people, each taken from their ordinary lives and thrust into a situation so extraordinary as to mark a generation. There were also those left behind: mothers, fathers, children, partners and friends. Many of those loved ones did not come home. Others returned with catastrophic mental and physical injuries; forever altered by their experiences, they were unable to relate to those at home. Many relatives never found out what happened to missing loved ones. They could not bring themselves to accept a pre-printed page with their loved one's name entered on it, coldly telling them that they were missing in action, taken prisoner, presumed dead, or killed.

This story is that of one family, and one particular soldier. It argues that stories such as this truly bring home the reality of the Great War. In learning the name – and the experiences – of just one, and knowing that many million experienced similar struggles, the true scale of the war is felt. Uniquely in this story is an insight into the lives of the many millions of wives and children who waited anxiously, desperately and fearfully for the delivery of the post.

There is a great body of literature on the First World War and many soldier's accounts survive. The imagery of this war has remained strong over one hundred years through photography, film, fiction, academic study, personal interest and contemporary memoirs, in addition to the permanent memorials on the landscape throughout the country. As well as official histories of the war, the experiences of all ranks have been portrayed, although that of the front-line soldier or 'Tommy' does seem the most prominent. The post-war literature stemmed from a need to explain, compare and make sense of what people had witnessed and experienced. Over the century more accounts from the Home Front, as well as women's work during the war, have added to the picture of life during the conflict. Whilst one family's account cannot be used to make any generalisations, it can add another strand to ever-increasing studies that explore experiences otherwise overlooked, forgotten, and in the case of these letters, very nearly lost.

---

1 For further reading on experiences from the Home Front during the First World War see I. Beckett, *Home Front 1914–1918: How Britain Survived the Great War* (London, 2006: The National Archives); S. Humphries and R. van Emden, *All Quiet on the Home Front: An Oral History of Life in Britain During the First World War* (London, 2004: Headline Publishing Group); A. Clare, *For King and Country: Calderdale's First World War Centenary 2014–2018* (Halifax, 2015: Calderdale Museums).

Numerous families kept soldiers' correspondence from the front, and many museum archives contain thousands of such letters. By contrast, the letters sent to soldiers are often lost, leaving fewer accounts of domestic life. However, this collection of Jack and Gert Adam provides insights into life at home: Jack sometimes wrote on the reverse of Gert's letters, and many letters from Gert were returned to her unopened. There are even letters between the children and their father. Of course, using letters to tell a story has its weaknesses. Not only can they be fragmentary, but both writers' thoughts can be self-censored, each wanting to reassure the recipient.[2] Letters home often disguised the true realities of the writer's experiences, which only personal diaries could recall. The letters in this volume are full of reassurances from both the soldier writing home and the family at home writing back. They offer reminders that while the war raged, life went on and children grew up while their father was away; everyday things still mattered and provided a focus away from the horrors of Jack's real daily experiences. Jack notes the similarity with letters home from his 'boys', as they too felt unable to explain to those at home the truth of their experiences and the fears they felt.

Jack and Gert's eloquent and heartfelt letters vividly captured their experiences either side of the 'water between' them: Jack's desire for life at home to remain unchanged, maintaining a recognisable sanctuary for his return, making the separation seem just temporary; Gert at home with the three young children, writing to Jack at every opportunity and encouraging the children to write to their father, knowing how much their letters will mean to him; Jack huddled in his cold quarters, artillery fire in the distance, writing merrily of his 'adventures' and longing to get home; Gert now sitting by the window waiting for the post delivery, anxious as always for news; and Jack left 'sitting on top of a shell-hole wounded in the knee',[3] wondering whether he would ever see his loved ones again. In the final months of the war Gert's letters to Jack were returned unopened and he was reported as missing in action. The collection reveals her anguish as she awaited news and her endeavours to find out exactly what had happened to her husband. Jack did not return. Gert did not receive official confirmation that he was killed until December 1919, long after the war was officially over.

The letters themselves have a remarkable story as they were lost in a house sale and purchased by the Royal Armouries Museum in 2006. The Royal Armouries is the national museum of arms and armour, originally based at the Tower of London. Although the primary focus is items relating to arms and armour, the museum also contains a range of archives including manuals, blueprints, photographs, personal letters and soldiers' diaries. At the time the letters were acquired, the Royal Armouries had a Writer in Residence, Peter Spafford, who started to look through them. Realising the poignancy of the story he decided to write the letters into a play, entitled 'Only Water Between' (a phrase taken from one of Jack's letters). After a performance it transpired that two of the couple's grandchildren were still living in the area and were delighted the letters had been found and their grandparents' story was being shared. They were able to fill in some of the gaps in the story and explain what happened to the family after the war. In 2009 the family discovered more letters to add to the collection.

2 Roper interestingly looks at the difference in content of soldiers' letters written to family and friends and also the importance of correspondence for soldier and family wellbeing: M. Roper, *The Secret Battle: Emotional Survival in the Great War* (Manchester, 2010: Manchester University Press).
3 Royal Armouries, ADAM A4/12, Gert Adam to the Queen Victoria Jubilee Fund Association, 27 August 1918.

2 Photograph of (left to right) Jack, Peg and Madge Adam. © Royal Armouries, ADAM B4/12.

CHAPTER ONE

THE EARLY YEARS OF THE WAR

John Gill Simpson Adam, known as Jack, was born on 30 July 1883, and Gertrude Marshall, known as Gert, was born on 22 October 1882. They were both born in Doncaster where Jack worked for a time at Balby Road School. He would have been twenty years old when the following reference was written, at the start of his career as a teacher. He already seems to have made a good impression on the headmaster:

> 'J. Adam is a teacher of considerable ability. He has taught at different times every standard in the school and at the time of leaving was in charge of strands VI and VII. He is able to take the Drawing and Geography of any of the classes and also the singing of any standard. Whilst a P.T. he always his examinations with credit and earned the Govt. Grants. He is 20 years of age and strong and healthy and with perseverance and attention should make a successful teacher.'[1]

Once married, the couple moved down to Highbury in North London for Jack to work at Drayton Park School. Jack was very active in teaching circles and on several committees.[2] The couple had three children: John William Marshall, also known as Jack, born in 1909, followed by Peggy in 1910 and Madge in 1912. When war broke out in 1914, the family were living in Highbury, London. Jack volunteered to serve in the British Army in March 1915 and joined the 12th Battalion, London Regiment in the early days of its formation. Because of his teaching background, he worked as a physical training instructor and was retained for the training of the drafts in England. Within two or three days he was promoted to Corporal, owing to his special ability in the teaching of physical exercises. In May 1915 he was made sergeant and by August he was promoted to Company Sergeant Major – a rapid rise through the ranks. A later reference on his military career said, 'His experience in teachers' organisations at home made him a very valuable asset to the whole battalion and in any re-shuffling of company commanders, there was always competition to get "Adam's Company".'[3]

---

1 Royal Armouries, ADAM A1/2, reference by W.I. Gundry, headmaster at Balby Road School, Doncaster, 21 July 1902.
2 Jack Adam was on the Committee of the London Teachers' Association, Secretary to the London Class Teachers' Association and a member of the Finsbury and City Local Council of the National Union of Teachers.
3 Royal Armouries, ADAM A4/31, reference by Mr. Brown, Col. Sgt., 12th London Regiment, about Jack Adam. Undated, but written after his death in 1918.

3 Jack Adam in uniform. © Royal Armouries. ADAM A5/1.

Whilst working in the south of England, it seems that Jack was able to make regular visits home, and that Gert and the children were able to visit him. Gert and the children then moved back up to Doncaster from Highbury at some point in the early years of the war to stay with her parents whilst he was away. Where Jack was stationed is not always clear but it seems that his locations throughout the war were Regents Park initially, and Tadworth from May 1915. He was in Richmond Park Camp in August 1915, Fovant, Salisbury from January to November 1916, Exeter from November 1916 to April 1917 and then at Deepcut, Aldershot until he was posted to France in January 1918.

The bulk of the archive collection consists of letters between Jack and Gert saved from when Jack was posted overseas in January 1918. Several letters in the collection were written by Jack to the children, and some of their letters to him also survive. Jack Junior, the eldest child, was five years old at the start of the war. Peggie, the middle child, would have been four, and Madge was still a toddler.

> Dear Peg, I am getting on very well. I have left London and come back to camp. I am very sorry about your cough, hope you will soon be better. Have you got a ball yet? I told Mr. Gardner about you wanting a hockey ball and he promised to look out, so perhaps it will come along after all. Hoping you will soon be better. I am your Daddie. I hope you have put the money in the war Loan.[4]

4 Royal Armouries, ADAM A2/77, undated letter from Jack Adam to Peg Adam, sent from Deepcut.

4 Postcard sent from Salisbury, postmarked 25 February 1916. The reverse reads 'Letter to follow. Firing all day just got back writing letter now. Doing well. Mother says you're going well.' Jack is in the middle row, fourth from left. ADAM B4/4.

Dear Peg, I have your letter which I think is very nice, particularly the stitching. Your writing is much improved. How do you like taking Madge to school? I hope you look after her but I know you will do. Mamma tells me you take her to Beechfield, that is very nice. It is raining very hard here and during the night the rain came through the roof by the side of my bed. Well goodbye, hope to hear again soon. Your Dad.[5]

At some point Jack did not receive Gert's letters and his concerns are echoed in his letters after hearing she had been taken ill. He writes to her from Salisbury:

'I felt just like a ship without a sail. Still after I saw and knew you were still alive and only wanted a little time to get better I felt considerably improved I have shed more tears over this than I have done since I was a boy. I missed you terribly and I wanted you badly. I never knew how dear you are to me till you were not there and it seemed awful.'[6]

Gert had been taken ill with Scarlet Fever but did make a recovery. Jack laments 'I wish I was with you', and confesses 'I am afraid if anything happened to you I should be a wash out while I remained behind', reminding us of the worries of those away from home for those left behind. 'I wish I could write nicer and longer letters. I could say a lot to you if I had my arm round you and was looking into your eyes and kissing you now and again.' It seems that baby Madge also caught Scarlet Fever and Jack writes to her too and says 'Well Mag, so you have got the scarlet fever too. Well! That is nice you will be able to sleep with Mammy and talk to her'. He finishes with a poem for Gert:

5 Royal Armouries, ADAM B2/2, undated letter from Jack Adam to Peg Adam.
6 Royal Armouries, ADAM B2/3, undated letter from Jack Adam to Gert Adam, sent from Salisbury.

That you have made the world a wondrous garden
Fair with the rose and glad with skies of blue
That you have wakened life's great song of gladness
Believe it true dear love believe it true

That I have found within that wondrous garden
All passing hours made beautiful and true
That my hearts prayer is God bless you ever
Believe it true I give my love to you
Believe it true I love I love but you

After years working for the Army in England, by January 1918, Jack was waiting to be deployed to France and the frustrations of waiting are evident. On 12 January Jack writes, 'Well things are just the same here. The battalion is at present at Bethune miles behind the line in barracks and will not probably be there till March. They went there on the 8th of Jan.' He finishes, 'Your own darling, Jack. Give my love to mother and father.'[7] The next day he states: 'Nothing happened of any importance today. After discussion I think it will be some 2 or 3 days before we move at all.' He bemoans that '[t]hings in the Battalion are very "empty" no organisation or anything and Poor Sam Brown is very sick of the whole shoot. I don't know what I shall do during the next 3 days hang around I suppose.' Clearly missing home and family he tells Gert that 'I thought as I came out of Church I would sooner be taking my 3 kiddies to see their Grandma'. Still waiting to be moved on 16 January Jack finishes his letter, 'Well I think there is nothing else darling just waiting. I wish I was waiting with you my own. Well Goodbye. Your Sweetheart. Jack.'[8]

7 Royal Armouries, ADAM A2/1, Jack Adam to Gert Adam, undated but envelope stamped 12 January 1918.
8 Royal Armouries, ADAM A2/5, Jack Adam to Gert Adam, undated but envelope stamped 16 January 1918.

CHAPTER TWO

'IT'S ONLY WATER BETWEEN'

After spending much of the war in England, Jack arrived in France at the end of January 1918 after waiting for some weeks to be deployed. He first served as Company Sergeant Major with the 1/6th London Regiment, then for a short time with the 1/12th and later with the 1/8th Battalion, Post Office Rifles.

Letters between Jack and Gert were sent back and forth almost daily. The surviving collection contains over seventy letters from Jack and there may have been others which were lost en route. The first letter written by Jack in France on 26 January, which no doubt Gert would have read anxiously, tells of his journey across the Channel.

> Well we went to the place I mentioned from Farnborough and got aboard at 4.30pm about 11,000 of us. A battalion and some bits. We started off later and racing across at what seemed a terrible rate for a ship. Landed at our destination early in the morning. It was interesting to watch our escort and the various tricks and dodges to get us safely across. It was a very clear night, quite the worse for our purpose. The decks were strewn, or packed rather, with men.[1]

Jack tells of '[a] very nice steam bath and dinner' on arrival and seeing an acquaintance Tom Turner 'sitting in this mess now. We recognised each other quickly.' As a teacher Jack knew many young men and recounts to Gert 'I have met quite a number of my old boys. Hardly off the ship before one rushed across.' Full of reassurances and cheerfulness he reports that 'We sleep in a tent tonight but it's a great adventure and very novel and interesting at present'. Unable to disclose much about his location and work, he asks Gert to 'Keep all my letters and I will tell you more when I see you'. With the couple now separated by the English Channel and with Jack closer to danger, his sign-off is poignant: the couple would never see each other again. 'Give my love to the kiddies. For yourself I have nothing left. You have everything but my actual presence and that, I trust, you will have for all time shortly. Well, Goodbye Darling. Your own Jack.'[2]

The next day he writes again:

> Still as before. Saturday morning 11.30am. Just had a glass of Horlicks malted at the YMCA for which I had to pay 20 centimes. Well I told you we have received a lot of stuff and now we have to draw a leather jacket. I think that perambulator would be very handy if I had it here. We slept very comfortably in the tent, quite warm, but some of the pictures are funny. Sewing buttons on by a candle which is stuck in your tin hat and somebody borrows the light to light his fag. They evidently expect us to be cold for we are supposed to have undershirt, shirt, cardigan, tunic,

---

1 Royal Armouries, ADAM A2/6, Jack Adam to Gert Adam, 26 January 1918.
2 Royal Armouries, ADAM A2/6, Jack Adam to Gert Adam, 26 January 1918.

and leather jacket and a waterproof which makes either a groundsheet or cloak. We intend to go to town tonight and to our regiment tomorrow as far as I know I think it's a long way off. Tell somebody to send me a 'lighter' same as mother gave me. The scarf is champion at night. I can't part my hair very well and it's cold but you get used to it. I am feeling champion at present and of course this is only a temporary arrangement. Know more about things when I get to the Battalion. Have met ever so many people I know.[3]

The letter has then been added to:

Afternoon. Yes we are off God knows where. There is enough stuff to carry as would sink a ship. One chap remarked 'Christ what shall I do with this lot?' Another boy replied 'Put it on the top of mine, just half a minute though! I've a piano to put on first.' One chap asked if he couldn't have a couple of tents to carry at the slope. They woke me up this morning at 5.20, and cold, by saying 'mother wants to know if you'll bring your slippers when you come down.' The spirits are grand it's one glorious adventure and joke all day. Of course, it will change no doubt, but I enjoy it splendidly.[4]

On 28 January Jack is on the move again and travels by train until 1 February to join his regiment. He writes to Gert, 'I'm still alive but not much kick. I rose rather early and have been on the move ever since. Tell Jack all the porters on the railway have penny trumpets to start the engine with and they don't move very quickly.' Keeping things light, Jack tells Gert, 'When we were all dressed up the Sergeant Major asked if we had forgot anything and one chap said 'yes' he'd left a chest of drawers behind'. He even quotes the letters his men are sending home: ' "Dear mother, This war is a b_ _ r send me some humbugs." Another one: "Dear Wife, Please send 10/- and the 'Christian Herald'. Don't forget the Christian Herald." Things go on charmingly and we laugh and joke the whole day through. There's no place like Blighty though. More later, Jack.'[5]

As well as hearing of Jack's experiences, letters from Gert show how she keeps Jack up to date on her life with the children back at home.

I am sitting in front of the fire with Madge on my knee. She is much better but still not up to concert pitch. Just been reading Tennyson's Dora to Peg and Madge. Now Peg has got the hymn book (Just gone over to give Jack's back a pat while he is coughing). Now they are wanting tea, so will go and get it ready. Peg just remarked this is the 'baddest' writing I have done – and no wonder.[6]

With Jack now in France, he continued to write and receive letters from his children as well.

From Daddy Adam. To my three Darlings: Jack, Peg, and Madge.

Still in the same place. Had a look around the town tonight. It's funny when you want something and can't ask for it. Everybody says S'il vous plait every time, which means If you Please.

We had to take our tent down this morning and just where I'd been sleeping was a ball of bits of paper and in the middle were three baby mice without any hair on. They are dead now.

Well, goodbye. I am going on a French train today and they are not half so nice as the English. Ta ta. Dad.[7]

3 Royal Armouries, ADAM A2/7, Jack Adam to Gert Adam, 27 January 1918.
4 Royal Armouries, ADAM A2/7, Jack Adam to Gert Adam, 27 January 1918.
5 Royal Armouries, ADAM A2/9–10, Jack Adam to Gert Adam, 28 January 1918.
6 Royal Armouries, ADAM A3/1, Gert Adam to Jack Adam, 21 January 1918.
7 Royal Armouries, ADAM A2/7, Jack Adam to Jack, Peg and Madge Adam, 27 January 1918.

By 5 February, Jack is now Company Sergeant Major with the 1/12th London Regiment in France. He is not being asked to do much at this stage and his letter reveals the state of the British military by this stage in the war. He discloses to Gert:

> I am still buckshee, which means a spare part. I do nothing practically all day. The officer said today they would probably send us all back to England but I do not think it is at all likely. They might send the chaps who have been here a long time but not me. I have met a lot of old comrades and the promotions out here are wicked. Men I had that I wouldn't trust 6*d* with have become CSMs. It seems here you get a stripe and wait till all the others get knocked out and you become CSM. Unless I am a perfect coward I don't fear my job. It seems a very safe one too. The 12ᵗʰ only lost one CSM during the last 12 months and he asked for it.[8]

There are many references in the letters to the difficulty of correspondence. On 8 February Jack writes, 'I am sweating on a letter from you I expect the first this afternoon at 3 o'clock.'[9] Considering that by August 1916 some 1.1 million letters were sent to the Western Front each day,[10] the occasional delays in sending and receiving letters is not surprising. This was clearly a source of much frustration and caused some confusion. A few days later on 11 February: 'Still no letter arrives. I have had the one from Elsie. I am getting quite anxious that no other has arrived. Of course there may not have been time for you to have written since I gave you my new address.'[11]

Jack receives word from Gert five days later and replies 'Well at last we are in touch and I have now received your letter written on Sunday last, the 10th. Of course, all that you have written before is German to me and I think you had better repeat the important parts. It seems to take four days to get a letter to England and five to get here. The time seems to depend on your officer censoring them.' Gert has updated him on the children and he replies, 'Peg evidently is very fond of church. I wish I could go to Balby Church. I can see myself singing in the village choir now.' Letters were an important respite from the work and dangers the soldiers faced and Jack optimistically states, 'I suppose you have given my address to everybody. So I am looking forward to a letter or two.' He still seems to be 'Buckshee' and tells her 'I have done one hour's work up to now. Had to drill a squad yesterday and I have to repeat the dose today.'[12] Jack remains positive and reassures Gert that he will manage to get home on leave. 'My chum's wife wrote to say that married soldiers are to have leave every six months and in that case I shall be home for my birthday. I hope so.'[13] His birthday was 30 July.

However, by 23 February Jack has not heard from Gert again and writes: 'Sweetheart, I am somewhat at a loss about your letters; they have suddenly ceased to arrive. I don't think I have had one since Tuesday at least. I had one from Mother yesterday.'[14] Two days later he hears from Gert: 'I had your letter yesterday in which you are so pleased we have got into communication. I am awaiting your long letter, which you promise. I think you have all my letters haven't you. All I am missing are those you sent at first.'[15]

---

8 Royal Armouries, ADAM A2/14, Jack Adam to Gert Adam, 5 February 1918.
9 Royal Armouries, ADAM A2/15, Jack Adam to Gert Adam, 8 February 1918.
10 R. van Emden, *The Quick and the Dead: Fallen Soldiers and Their Families in the Great War* (London, 2011: Bloomsbury), 44.
11 Royal Armouries, ADAM A2/16, Jack Adam to Gert Adam, 11 February 1918.
12 Royal Armouries, ADAM A2/17, Jack Adam to Gert Adam, 16 February 1918.
13 Royal Armouries, ADAM A2/18, Jack Adam to Gert Adam, 16 February 1918.
14 Royal Armouries, ADAM A2/21, Jack Adam to Gert Adam, 23 February 1918.
15 Royal Armouries, ADAM A2/22, letter from Jack Adam to Gert Adam, 27 February 1918.

The postal service was a lifeline for both those serving overseas and those at home. Awaiting the daily delivery at home or in the field would have been anxious, days at a time spent with no news. As van Emden suggests, 'If anything, it was easier not to receive a letter on a regular basis as a lengthy silence was not then misinterpreted as something ominous.'[16] On 21 February Jack has mentioned that 'things are still "as you were" but I must write because I suppose if I miss a day or so I shall have departed this life'.[17] On the same day, Gert reveals how desperate she was to hear from Jack and how much his apparent silence affected everyday life – anxiety doubtless shared by countless other families in similar circumstances:

> Oh Jack, how glad I am we have got in touch at last – made one begin to feel desperate. Yes I think it takes about four days for your letters to reach me.
>
> This one was written on the 16th, got here this morning 21st. Busy morning boy so will write after dinner and send by this even post.
>
> Can't wait till afternoon – feel I must just let a little steam off. I heard too that leave is to be every six months for married soldiers, nine for single men. Oh boy it's too intoxicating to think of! It is so lovely to think you will really get my letters now; it puts some heart into me. Jack, I've written and written – smiles and tears, but I feel jubilant this morning.
>
> Mother is very glad you are getting plenty of food. She has been busy preparing pickles for when you come home. We get what we need. The worst is the standing for it. Mother was an hour and a half getting suet this morning. She is always thinking about you.
>
> You will know by Jack's letters he is in good spirits and going to school. Peg too is merry and bright. I think she has a daily practise on the trapezes at the Shakespeare drinking fountain. She does seem strong. She was taking the market men off last night. You would have rocked with laughter to hear her. Then she was Jack's horse. It was a wet night and they had to give vent to their energy indoors. I have a fire every day in the front room and they play nicely there, or knit or draw.
>
> I will send the diary off tomorrow. Goodbye till then. Your Own Darling[18]

Jack's reply reassures her and mentions her having to wait for food.

> I get your letters and they will follow me now.
>
> Nothing to get desperate about, I can carry on my present job for duration. Yes, the leave is nice, but I am afraid "military contingencies" will not allow it when the time comes. Let's hope they will. Bravo! for the pickles. Yes you've "written and written" and incidentally I have not done bad have I? I don't see any necessity for tears, should be all smiles, it is with me.
>
> I am sorry about the standing for food. I don't like that and am very sorry for Mother. Give her my love.
>
> Tell Peg Dad used to swing on the same bar when he was a boy and I should very much like to have heard her taking off the market men.
>
> It's a good idea to take them in the room. All you want there is a piano.
>
> I am expecting a diary and a long letter today.
>
> I think there is nothing else darling. God bless you all. Your Sweetheart[19]

16 Van Emden, *The Quick and the Dead*, 36.
17 Royal Armouries, ADAM A2/20, Jack Adam to Gert Adam, 21 February 1918.
18 Royal Armouries, ADAM A2/22, Gert Adam to Jack Adam, 21 February 1918.
19 Royal Armouries, ADAM A2/22, Jack Adam to Gert Adam, 26 February 1918.

As the war continued, Jack lost a friend and shared with Gert that 'I am very sorry I have lost my chum, he was a very intelligent chap and we had many happy hours together'.[20] He encloses a letter to Peg in the same envelope, a note which could have been written by any father in any circumstances over the last century, but made more touching knowing Jack was heading to the frontlines and had just lost a friend:

Dear Peg. I suppose you are well. I hope so at any rate. How's school going? Do you get on well there? How's Grandma and Aunt Elsie – I hear Uncle Harry was over at Whitsuntide. I am very sorry that it rained and spoiled the picnic. Still there will be many fine days before you grow up to be a woman. Well, keep on playing about and send me a note now and again. Your Dad.[21]

Although Jack tries to maintain his cheery tone and optimism to reassure Gert back home, by March his reflections on events reveal his longing for home. Jack confesses 'It made me nearly cry to see so many marching in the other day'.[22] A week later he writes, 'I had a look at the boat which takes you to Blighty but nobody would let me on'.[23] On 13 March Jack writes, 'It's a glorious morning and I am sitting outside the tent writing this. Of course, we are an hour in front of you. The French put their clocks on at 2am March 9th so anybody going home now gains an hour. I suppose all the clocks will be synchronised by the time I get home in July'.[24] His hope to get leave after six months in France is still evident: 'We went down to Le Havre again yesterday. Boys keep coming in and going out some in from the line others from England and they both pass here. I could see England from the shore.' In the same letter, always full of stories from the other men, Jack retells how a '[c]hap here just showing us the newspaper, which came while he was on leave, in which he is shown "Seriously wounded", and a paper a week earlier showing him "Dead of wounds"! He is very much alive.'[25]

Gert's letters often share her and her mother's concerns over food. Rationing was introduced in 1917 and must have caused a great strain on a mother with three young children to feed. On 16 February Jack tells her 'yes you can manage with vegetables, the French in all the parts I have seen live on nothing else. The difficulty of looking after the allotment will be the worst'.[26] On 19 February he mentions the food again in his letter: 'I think the rationing will be better. We are alright and want nothing. I am sorry you are all so short of food. That is to say as things go. There is plenty of fresh butter here; I wish I could get it across. Here we are alright. I have my food today in sufficiency'.[27] Furthermore, Gert was also now responsible for the family finances and Jack instructs her on 23 February what separation allowance she should be entitled to.[28]

As well as matters of food, money and the children, the couple's letters reveal their own longings and desires. Jack's letters include 'I think we shall have another honeymoon'.[29] 'Frisky? I like that at your age. Why you're an old married woman; at least your husband's

20 Royal Armouries, ADAM A2/24, Jack Adam to Gert Adam, 3 March 1918.
21 Royal Armouries, ADAM A2/24, Jack Adam to Gert Adam, 3 March 1918.
22 Royal Armouries, ADAM A2/26, Jack Adam to Gert Adam, 4 March 1918.
23 Royal Armouries, ADAM A2/28, Jack Adam to Gert Adam, 10 March 1918.
24 Royal Armouries, ADAM A2/29, Jack Adam to Gert Adam, 13 March 1918.
25 Royal Armouries, ADAM A2/29, Jack Adam to Gert Adam, 13 March 1918.
26 Royal Armouries, ADAM A2/18, Jack Adam to Gert Adam, 16 February 1918.
27 Royal Armouries, ADAM A2/19, Jack Adam to Gert Adam, 19 February 1918.
28 Royal Armouries, ADAM A2/21, Jack Adam to Gert Adam, 23 February 1918.
29 Royal Armouries, ADAM A2/26, Jack Adam to Gert Adam, 4 March 1918.

an old married man.'[30] 'Of course, the best for yourself. I wish I could give it to you. Well we shall someday and it will be nice, but I am getting too old for sweethearting you know.'[31]

During the months Jack is in France clearly Gert is worried, especially with Jack moving ever nearer to danger. On 4 March he talks of the 'music' (meaning the artillery fire): 'Very little happening here except music, which has been very loud of late, this morning particularly.'[32] A letter on 9 March from Gert reads 'My dear Jack, I could only make guesses at the place you have been in. I sincerely hope you are moving back. The nearer you are to England the better will suit me.'[33]

The couple's hope was always for Jack to be given leave, or moreover, the war to be over. On 13 March Jack is clearly frustrated and doesn't want Gert to get her hopes up:

'Well after a journey I have got to the same place as I started from - almost the same tent. Of course, it's very questionable what is going to happen. I certainly don't think we shall be here many days. I have met lots of people I know. Of course, I know what you would like, and you may think it, but I am afraid you'll be disappointed. Of course, there are rumours, but I won't say any more. I am afraid that is impossible.'[34]

On 18 March Jack tells Gert, 'Another absurd rumour came in. It would please you - well I shall hear this week I hope. Don't say anything to anyone it's too absurd.'[35] Five days later Jack has heard he 'may be shifting', potentially nearer to home or even back to England. He continues, 'Don't hope darling for fear of disappointment. The betting here is even money. It's too good so don't think about it and don't tell anybody.'[36] However, just a few days later he reports 'The offensive having started I am afraid we shall be kept back till it settles down a bit. I suppose you will read it in the papers if it is so. I had hopes of being home by Easter but I am afraid it is impossible now and nobody knows what will happen. A chap in the next tent got on to the boat to go home, was brought back, and today goes to Italy.'[37]

The long years of wartime had taken their toll on the nation and individuals. Whilst Jack had remained safely in England during most of the war training recruits, it did mean by the time he was posted overseas to join the frontline, he and Gert were well aware of the situation – the high death toll and poor conditions that filtered through the newspapers, letters home, and (in time) film and photography. They also probably feared that another 'big push' must be on its way to break the endless stalemate on the Western Front, this time with Jack right in the middle of it.

Jack's letter to Gert on 28 March dashes both of their hopes for a reunion at Easter.

30 Royal Armouries, ADAM A2/31, Jack Adam to Gert Adam, undated letter 'Friday Teatime', most likely from March 1918.
31 Royal Armouries, ADAM A2/34, Jack Adam to Gert Adam, 21 March 1918.
32 Royal Armouries, ADAM A2/26, Jack Adam to Gert Adam, 4 March 1918.
33 Royal Armouries, ADAM A3/2, Gert Adam to Jack Adam, 9 March 1918.
34 Royal Armouries, ADAM A2/30, Jack Adam to Gert Adam, 13 March 1918.
35 Royal Armouries, ADAM A2/32, Jack Adam to Gert Adam, 18 March 1918.
36 Royal Armouries, ADAM A2/35, Jack Adam to Gert Adam, 23 March 1918.
37 Royal Armouries, ADAM A2/36, Jack Adam to Gert Adam, 26 March 1918. Operation Michael was Germany's last great onslaught of the war, the first phase of a move designed to drive the British from the Somme and the French from the Aisne before sufficient American troops arrived to affect the outcome. Described by Churchill as 'the greatest onslaught in the history of the world', the Spring Offensive was a short period of incredible ferocity that saw the German army reach within forty miles of Paris before falling back.

The order is cancelled and that's all we know. It's been a terrible struggle according to the papers but there is a confidence about it all, and directly the hour will arrive for the counter attack, and although I can't see getting all the land back, I think the fate of the German is sealed. Keep a lot of peace and quiet at home and victory is ours. German money fell yesterday, which is one of the surest signs of the times.[38]

He adds, 'By the way, I am dead and buried according to Deepcut. Boys coming out here are surprised to see me.'[39]

The couple often wrote on the back of each other's letters and on the reverse of Jack's letter of 20 July 1918, had been a letter from Gert dated 10 April 1918, a letter he had kept, but used when short of paper. Gert's letter in April shows their letters were being delayed. 'Dear Jack, Hope I shall have a letter this morning. Have heard nothing since the post Saturday morning. No fresh news I think from this side. All goes along as usual. Kiddies just gone to school. Hope you are still "as you were".'[40] Her comment is a reminder of how little Jack could tell her of what he was really up to. 'What am I doing? Oh the usual leaning up against the wall.'[41]

On Easter Sunday, still in France, Jack writes, 'Of course you know by now what happened to all the surplus senior ranks. 52 of us were ordered to proceed to Blighty and we quite expected to be home by Easter. However, [it was] intervened and we were ordered to be reposted. We were asked individually what Battalions we desired to join. I chose 1/12. In fact, all our boys did. Now what will happen we don't know.' He reassures Gert that 'I am safe, you are safe, the kiddies are well. As I sit on the floor of this tent writing I am looking at the River Seine and the sun is shining beautifully.' He finishes the letter by signing 'J G ADAM', before realising and putting 'Sorry, Jack.'[42] Obviously he is in the habit of signing official documents as much as writing home.

In April Jack is moved again and can only tell Gert that 'My number appears again and I move tomorrow. I don't know where to. Sufficient that we all go together. I will write as soon as I know anything.'[43] A week later a brief letter simply states 'Somewhere. Anywhere. Don't know the day. Don't know where. It's Tuesday I think. If it's a Tuesday it's the 16th April.'[44] A few days later on the 19th, Jack tells Gert:

Well it's the longest period elapsed since writing. I travelled to here with 2000 other men, then were all divided up and I have had two companies in three days and I have been very busy. We are in tents and it's damnably cold. In fact, I spend most miserable nights. However, it's better than another place. We are in no danger, although we hear the music.[45]

A much longer and more detailed letter is written by Jack on 21 April, full of frustration and unable to give any details on where he is or what was likely to happen next. The next day his letter is gentler, and he tells Gert of a dream where 'I had a quarrel with you last night but it was before we were married. You allied yourself with a party who were against me.

38 Royal Armouries, ADAM A2/37, Jack Adam to Gert Adam, 28 March 1918.
39 Royal Armouries, ADAM A2/37, Jack Adam to Gert Adam, 28 March 1918.
40 Royal Armouries, ADAM B2/16, Gert Adam to Jack Adam, 10 April 2018. Jack's letter dated 20 July 1918 is written on the reverse.
41 Royal Armouries, ADAM B2/8, Jack Adam to Gert Adam, 17 June 1918.
42 Royal Armouries, ADAM A2/39, Jack Adam to Gert Adam, dated Easter Sunday [31 March] 1918.
43 Royal Armouries, ADAM A2/43, Jack Adam to Gert Adam, 8 April 1918.
44 Royal Armouries, ADAM A2/46, Jack Adam to Gert Adam, envelope dated 16 April 1918.
45 Royal Armouries, ADAM A2/47, Jack Adam to Gert Adam, 19 April 1918.

5 A drawing by Jack of his dugout for Peg. © Royal Armouries. ADAM A2/81.

I fought hard and finally I won. One of the girls in your party wanted to marry me but you rushed in (fancy you rushing!) and claimed me and you were very flushed when you did it. However, I woke up.'[46]

By the end of April, Jack is with the 12th London Regiment, 58 Divisional Wing, and men from the regiment were being called up to the front. He tells Gert that 'in two days three, no! four of our boys have gone up, so out of the eight senior ranks there are four of us left'. He ends, 'They keep going up one by one, and I suppose my turn will come eventually, meanwhile we carry on here'.[47]

By June 1918, after five months apart, Jack is writing home from the frontline trying to reassure Gert: 'I wish your spirit was as good as mine. The danger is small unless you go over, and I am not likely to do that. Don't worry.' He explains to Gert what he is up to: 'There appears to be two states, in and out. Out comes very rarely and is called rest. From "rest" you go in first to the outer zone and then a little nearer until you must reach the front, but having seen it you go back by stages to where you started from.'[48] Just a few days later he writes: 'There seems to be no actual 'out' at present for anybody', and adds, 'The war will end but when I can't say.'[49]

46 Royal Armouries, ADAM A2/49, Jack Adam to Gert Adam, 22 April 1918.
47 Royal Armouries, ADAM A2/52, Jack Adam to Gert Adam, 27 April 1918.
48 Royal Armouries, ADAM A2/55, Jack Adam to Gert Adam, 9 June 1918.
49 Royal Armouries, ADAM A2/57, Jack Adam to Gert Adam, 12 June 1918.

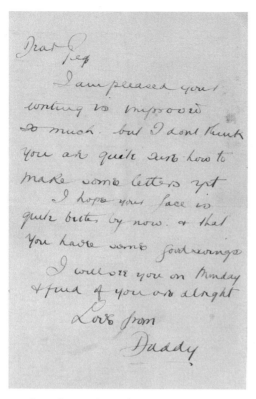

6 A letter from Jack to Peg. ADAM A2/76.

Jack is transferred into the Post Office Rifles on 16 June and sends a note to let Gert know, but once again – indicated by a remark the following day – their letters seem to be delayed: 'Letters may be a little disconnected and this incoherent'.[50] Jack tells Gert on 22 June that he 'went for a walk this afternoon into a village between us and Jerry and it was a sight to see the place all blown to bits, churches and all the lot. There was a baby doll in one house. Beautiful oak sideboards and furniture all broken some intact. Could furnish a beautiful house with what I saw. It was a funny thing the last house I was in – in the hall was an empty tin of Nuttall's Mintoes Doncaster on it.'[51]

The collection contains a small flower attached to a piece of card. Jack's letter of 17 June explains their origin: 'Poor old Madge gets tired does she the darling. I'll just get out and get her a flower from the back of the trenches – wait a moment – There! The yellow for Madge and Cornflower for Peg and the other blue for Jack and tell them they are grown just behind the trench "Somewhere in France"'.[52]

On 23 June, Jack is once again full of reassurances for Gert, but his mention of forgetting being married must have been hard for Gert to hear.

50 Royal Armouries, ADAM B2/8, Jack Adam to Gert Adam, 17 June 1918.
51 Royal Armouries, ADAM A2/63, Jack Adam to Gert Adam, 21 June 1918.
52 Royal Armouries, ADAM A2/82, flower on card with 'Somewhere in France' written above, June 1918.

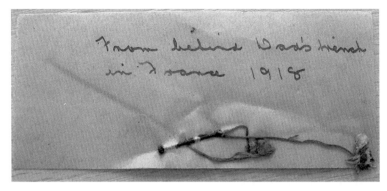

7 A pressed flower Jack sent to his children from France. © Royal Armouries. ADAM A2/82.

Things are going nicely here. This is a good dug-out but very low.

I hear leave will start again in 1919. My chum says that as the birth-rate is declining, soldiers are to be allowed home every Saturday night. What hopes. I want you very hard sometimes but not in that sense. Lately in fact I forget sometimes I am married. Yes, I remember you calling on the way upstairs. I wish I could hear you now. Goodbye. Your darling.[53]

At the end of June, Jack replies to Gert that he 'just got your letter. I am fine and the weather is splendid. Sitting in the open writing this.' She must have told him about young Jack and he comments 'So Jack couldn't get a job as a cattle driver? I wish I had been there. I would have got one for him. Never mind I'll look after him one day.'[54]

By July, Jack seems to be ever more tired and despite his generally optimistic tone, his true feelings come through about his desire to see her. 'I wanted you this morning very badly. Quite a long time since I felt like that. Got very tired this morning. It's not very nice standing looking at a trench wall for hours.' But always wanting to be positive for Gert he adds, 'Still, it's very nice when you wake up in a morning and the sun is shining and all is quiet. Give my love to the kiddies and mother.' He finishes poignantly with 'Goodbye darling. You are always with me. Jack.' He later adds more to the letter, revealing his longing for home, 'I often think in the night when we stand in the trench looking at the wall about you sleeping away. And the kiddies. I can see you, everyone in your own particular positions.'[55]

It is in this letter Jack mentions sending his old cap badge from the Rangers to Jack Junior.

Jack's closeness to danger and increasing activity on the Western Front are evident in several Field Service Postcards sent home in July.[56] Designed to be sent by soldiers on the move or on the frontline, they were a quick way to reassure those at home. They were called a 'Whizz Bang' or a 'Quick Five' and millions were sent home. Gert received Field Service postcards from Jack, all completed with the same information to say 'I am quite well', 'Letter

53 Royal Armouries, ADAM A2/64, Jack Adam to Gert Adam, 23 June 1918.
54 Royal Armouries, ADAM A2/67, Jack Adam to Gert Adam, 29 June 1918.
55 Royal Armouries, ADAM A2/69, Jack Adam to Gert Adam, 3 July 1918.
56 Royal Armouries, ADAM A2/70–76, Field Service postcards, Jack Adam to Gert Adam, dated 3, 4, 7, 9, 10, 11, 17 and 18 July 1918. The Allied counter-offensive began in mid-July, as the well-supplied and reinforced British, French and American troops began to overwhelm the declining Central Powers.

8 Jack's cap badge sent home for his son. © Royal Armouries. ADAM A1/8.

follows at first opportunity', and signed 'J G S Adam'. These were sent on the 3rd, 4th, 7th, 9th, 10th and 11th July, and again on 17th and 18th July.

The line 'I am quite well' simply means 'I am alive' and was often all those at home needed to know. They could also be an easy option to send home when one didn't know what to say. 'The implicit optimism of the post card is worth noting.'[57] It can only be filled in with a name, date and one option of either the optimistic 'I am quite well' or 'Been admitted to hospital'. There was no room for anything in between. 'I am quite well' was all that Gert, and many thousands of wives and families, were ever informed. After hearing regular news from Jack, to merely receive a series of field service postcards and inconsistent letters must have made Gert very anxious.

In the collection as it stood in 2006 were several Field Service postcards and one or two letters with overlapping dates, but very little other correspondence from June and July. However, those letters did refer to others that had been written, giving the impression that these might have been lost en route or not kept. Many of the extracts in this chapter were from letters found later, but included here to complete the story of Jack's service in France.

As July progresses, when he does have time to write, Jack seems ever more disheartened. He is unable to hide it from Gert. On 8 July, finally able to write more than a pre-printed postcard, Jack writes, 'Well we are still alive and kicking but the kick is very feeble. I am tired. Another man gone on leave this morning I suppose that's upset me. Still I suppose I shall come to my turn directly. I shall be pleased when this tour of duty is over I am getting

57 P. Fussell, *The Great War and Modern Memory* (Oxford, 1975: Oxford University Press), 185.

NOTHING is to be written on this side except the date and signature of the sender. Sentences not required may be erased. If anything else is added the post card will be destroyed.

[Postage must be prepaid on any letter or post card addressed to the sender of this card.]

I am quite well.

I have been admitted into hospital

{ sick } and am going on well.
{ wounded } and hope to be discharged soon.

I am being sent down to the base.

I have received your { letter dated_____
{ telegram „ _____
{ parcel „ _____

Letter follows at first opportunity.

I have received no letter from you

{ lately.
{ for a long time.

Signature }
only }

Date____10/9/1918____

(94800) Wt. W1566-R1619 14,000m. 6/17. J.J.K. & Co., Ltd.

9 One of several Field Service postcards Gert received from Jack. © Royal Armouries. ADAM A2/74.

fed up.' He adds: 'I am afraid I am a bit low spirits this morning. Au Revoir. God bless You. I wish your head was on my shoulder.'[58]

Over the next few days, Jack goes to the frontlines again. Once back in the reserve trenches he writes to Gert: 'I am alive and kicking. I have your letters and am sorry to hear about Jack being so ill. I hope he will soon be alright. Tell him Daddie is very tired. We haven't had much sleep lately but hope to have a day or two now. I saw a couple of our enemies the other day in fact I have spent a few days right in front. It's not nice but still it might be worse. I'll tell you all about it another day.' In the same letter he writes to his son, 'Cheer up Jack you'll soon be better and it's better being ill in a nice bed than going up a

58 Royal Armouries, ADAM B2/12, Jack Adam to Gert Adam, 8 July 1918.

trench and Jerry's bumping it. That's when you say your prayers.'[59] It is noticeable, perhaps inevitable, that his experiences, and the distance from his family, are affecting his reactions to news from home.

The next day, he writes more positively again, but can't hide the true meaning of having a 'splendid time': 'Of course you can guess where we have just come from. We had a splendid time and no one is any worse for the adventure.' He reports of his change of number and regiment too, 'I have been allotted a new number, 388027, so I suppose I belong to the Post Office Rifles forever.'[60]

At this time (late July 1918) the collection of letters become quite fragmented. The couple evidently remained in contact, since Gert's letters, such as this one written on 25 July, refer to recent letters received from Jack:

> Dear Jack, I've just got your long letter written last Sunday 21st. I have not stopped to digest it because I want to post this early in the hopes of your getting it on your birthday. We hoped once there would be no need to write, but one does not dare to hope too much for leave. I try not to think about it; except in a remote sort of way. Are there any hopes – say anywhere near? But I expect one has to wait ones turn. Well, at least if you cannot get home I hope you will get a long rest far away from the line. Darling I do wish 'Many Happy Returns' and a long Return, and all my love. Ever Your Gert[61]

It was a letter Jack never received.

59 Royal Armouries, ADAM B2/13, Jack Adam to Gert Adam, 13 July 1918.
60 Royal Armouries, ADAM B2/14, Jack Adam to Gert Adam, 14 July 1918.
61 Royal Armouries, ADAM A3/4, Gert Adam to Jack Adam, 25 July 1918.

CHAPTER THREE

MISSING IN ACTION

It transpired that Jack's battalion carried out a daylight raid on 25 July, and Jack did not return. He was known to have been wounded but no one could say exactly what happened next. Gert knew nothing of this, and continued to write to him regularly. She would not have received anything from him after 26 July, which would have left her concerned, but it was more than a week later, after 4 August, that her own letters, and those from the children, began to be returned.

Gert's letter written to Jack on his birthday, 30 July 1918, the day which they had once hoped he would be home, was returned, stamped 'present location unknown'. She had written, 'It's your birthday night, 10.30, and from a weather point of view it has been a lovely day. I will get your paper off tomorrow and this letter. I've had a very busy day today.' She had not heard from Jack for a while: 'Well, I hope your day has been as happy as possible. I got your field card of the 24th, so by now you may be out. I hope so. Well, goodnight Jack. Your Darling.' Another concern for Gert is her mother's health as she writes in the same letter that 'Mother has been very poorly and had to go to bed at last – has had pains, but I'm hoping a rest in bed will set her up.'[1]

Another letter from Gert on 1 August 1918 was also later returned to her. 'Dear Jack I'm here and almost ready for dropping off to sleep but I wonder where you are? Perhaps I shall hear something in the morning. I hope you are still going well.' She speaks of an end to the war, which was in discussion at this stage. 'The war news continues to be good and I think the big strike is settled up in some way. Some people think the war is nearing the end. It's just dreadful for people to keep on being slaughtered, but I suppose it will probably be ended by other means than fighting.' She ends by saying, 'Shall wait for the post before sending. She has just passed. Hope I'll hear something this afternoon. Best Love.'[2]

After having several letters returned to her and receiving nothing since the Field Service postcard on 25 July, Gert finally hears news on 9 August that Jack is injured. The letter itself is not in the collection, but Gert's immediate reply remains: 'My Dear Jack, I am sending this in the hope and prayer that you will be able to read and answer it. I heard this morning you had been wounded and Darling it has been one of the black days of my life. If it's only a scrawl in answer I will thank God for it. Your most anxious Gert.' Not knowing if Jack would receive this she wrote in the margin, 'I have no particulars should be very grateful for information from anyone.'[3] The letter was again later returned unopened and stamped 'Present Location Uncertain'.

1 Royal Armouries, ADAM A3/6, Gert Adam to Jack Adam, 30 July 1918.
2 Royal Armouries, ADAM A3/7, Gert Adam to Jack Adam, 1 August 1918.
3 Royal Armouries, ADAM A3/8, Gert Adam to Jack Adam, 9 August 1918.

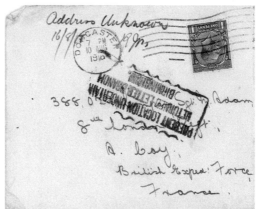

10 A letter from Gert to Jack, later returned to her. © Royal Armouries. ADAM A3/9.

With no news as to his whereabouts Gert continued to write to Jack each day, desperately hoping he was only wounded and would want to keep hearing from her. Her anxiety was clear, as can be felt in her letter dated 10 August.

> My Dear Jack. I feel I must keep writing. I trust you will get the letters.
>
> If I just get a word I'll be most thankful. I think I must still have a hope that all is well or I don't know how I should bear it. I have my information that you are wounded from the hospital. Your batman says he missed you 'after the scrap' but was told by some other fellows you were wounded in the knee. My heart feels almost broken and I pray for just a word of assurance. Ever your Darling. The Kiddies are all well. They are like I am – wanting Daddie very badly.[4]

A letter from Jack Junior posted on 24 July was also returned unopened. Nine-year-old Jack had written, 'Dear Daddy. It is a long time since I wrote to you last. I am sending you a map of England. I have drawn it all myself. I get on very well at school. I can do the sums all right. How are you getting on? I hope you are all right.'[5] Gert now, like so many mothers, was charged with reassuring the children that Daddy was safe, whilst not knowing herself.

From a later history of the Post Office Rifles, 8th Battalion, City of London Regiment,[6] and correspondence between Gert and other soldiers in his regiment, it transpired that Jack

---

4 Royal Armouries, ADAM A3/9, Gert Adam to Jack Adam, 10 August 1918. A 'batman' was a soldier assigned to an officer as their assistant.

5 Royal Armouries, ADAM A3/4, Jack Adam Junior to Jack Adam, 23 July 1918.

6 By July, Jack was serving with the Post Office Rifles, 8th Battalion.

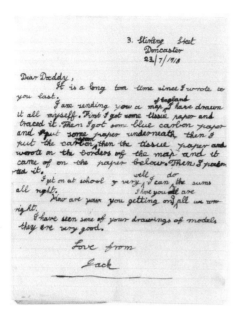

11 A letter from Jack Junior with a map he drew for his father, which was returned unopened.
© Royal Armouries. ADAM A3/3.

had been involved in a daylight raid on 25 July, five days before his birthday.[7] Jack did not return from the raid and for a considerable time there was such disarray that no one could account for his whereabouts. As Gert had been told, he had been wounded, but no one could say exactly what happened next.

The remainder of the letters in the collection reveal Gert's endeavours to find out exactly what happened to Jack.

After hearing on 9 August that he was injured, Gert had written to the War Office seeking information. She continued to write to Jack, hoping he was just in hospital or possibly taken prisoner and that the letters would eventually find him. Sadly, she was only ever to hear ever more discouraging reports about that fateful daylight raid, from which Jack would never return. A Post Office telegram dated 31 August 1918 simply reads 'Regret Sergeant Major Adam reported missing since 25.7.18 forward authority for report of death quote casualties 702557 War Office.'[8]

On 27 August, having heard nothing from Jack for over a month, Gert had written to the Secretary of the Queen Victoria Jubilee Fund Association for information. Her understated 'I am very troubled' masks a whirlwind of emotions.

> Dear Sir, I should be very grateful for any information you could give me regarding my husband No.388027 Rank Coy. Sgt. Maj., Name J. G. S. Adam. London Regiment A Company. I have had no news from him since a field card dated July 24th. He was seen sitting on the top of a shell-hole wounded in the knee and then lost sight of. He has been officially reported

7 Imperial War Museum, *History of the Post Office Rifles, 8th Battalion City of London Regiment 1914–1918* (London, 1997: Imperial War Museum).

8 Royal Armouries, ADAM A4/1, telegram from the War Office to Gert Adam, 31 August 1918.

'missing'. I am very troubled. I should be so thankful if I could know he was a prisoner of war. Thanking you in anticipation. I am Yours Truly. G. Adam.[9]

This letter was returned nearly a month later, stamped in Geneva on 7 September 1918, and in London on 23 September. Gert did get a reply from Geneva on 13 September though: 'In reply to your enquiry concerning: Adam C. Sgt. M. 388027 London Rgt. we herewith beg to inform you that his name has not yet appeared on the Lists of Prisoners, received from Germany. When it does so, we shall let you know as soon as possible.' The letter also states, 'As we find that many enquirers forward us photographs of their missing relatives or friends, we would mention that these are of no use to us in our investigations.'[10] It is a blunt reflection of families' desperation for news and the sheer size of the job keeping track of prisoners and locating missing men.

Gert also began corresponding with members of Jack's regiment, but only received piece-meal evidence about what may have happened. Several letters arrived between September to December 1918, each one dashing her hopes still further. A letter from the Commanding Officer of the 8th London Regiment shows not only that Gert received no final answers as to what happened to Jack – and actually gave her false hopes that he may have been taken prisoner – but also that her letters did not always get through to their destination.

> Dear Mrs. Adam, Your registered letter dated Sept 9th duly received yesterday – I regret no trace can be found of your former letter. I regret very much that I cannot give you any definite information about your husband. Every enquiry has been made and I am afraid it is more than probable that he was killed – but no one actually saw him killed nor was his body found, and as some prisoners were captured it is quite possible that he was amongst them. All the information we have been able to collect has been too uncertain to say definitely that he was killed – so I hope that you may shortly hear he is a prisoner in Germany. It takes a long time to get a letter through and it is more than possible you would not have heard yet. You have my sincerest sympathy in this matter and I much regret not being able to help you more.[11]

Another account, this time from the Regiment's Chaplain in October, unable to provide any further information, at least shared with her a memory of Jack, and again reveals the chaos at the front when dealing heavy death tolls: 'I may add that I saw your husband only a few moments before he went over and that I marvelled at the cheerfulness and confidence which prevailed generally in spite of the coming ordeal'. The writer concludes, 'You have the sincere sympathy of all out here in this very trying time – even though we are too occupied to write much – our casualties have been so numerous in the last few months that it has been impossible to deal with each one as we should have liked to do – and in many cases there has been a complete absence of any information whatsoever'.[12]

On 19 November, in the week following the general armistice on the Western Front, Gert received the following:

9 Royal Armouries, ADAM A4/12, Gert Adam to the Queen Victoria Jubilee Fund Association, 27 August 1918.

10 Royal Armouries, ADAM A4/14, Comite International De La Croix-Rouge: Agence Internationale Des Prisoners De Guerre to Gert Adam, 13 September 1918.

11 Royal Armouries, ADAM A4/19, Commanding Officer of the 8th London Regiment [signature illegible] to Gert Adam, 17 September 1918.

12 Royal Armouries, ADAM A4/23, Howard James, Chaplain, 8th London Regiment to Gert Adam, 4th October 1918.

We regret to say that we have received another very discouraging report about your husband from Private MacPhail 48818, who states that he saw your husband lying severely wounded in the leg in an enemy trench to the north of Albert on July 25th. He states that he heard Captain Poulton ask him if he could get back and your husband replied that he would try, but Private MacPhail does not know what became of him subsequently. We greatly fear that your husband met with some further disaster after he was seen by Private MacPhail, but we are continuing our enquiries in every direction on your behalf.[13]

The official report from the history of the Post Office Rifles, 8th Battalion, City of London Regiment states what happened on that day:

On July 25th a daylight raid on a large scale was carried out, about three hundred men going over the top. The raid met with little opposition on the front attacked, except in the neighbourhood of the Quarry where some platoons of A Company had a very hard time. A few prisoners were brought back and many more in attempting to escape had to be shot. But during the return journey the raiders received heavy machine-gun fire from the flanks of the attack, and suffered heavily. On the whole it seems probable that the casualties on both sides were about equal.[14]

When the war ended on 11 November 1918, Gert still did not know the fate of her husband. She now had the responsibility of explaining to her children, now aged nine, eight and six that the fighting had finished but she did not know when – if at all – their father would return. The grief of wives and families whose loved ones had fallen in battle provided a dramatic contrast with the celebrations as men returned each day from the front. Many solders remained overseas long after November 1918, but with war over, the feeling of relief that they were in less danger must have been a great comfort to those back home. Similarly, knowing a husband had been killed lent pity and support to women. For Gert, caught between possible relief that Jack may have been on his way back to her, and fear that she would never see him again, the uncertainty must have been unbearable. Every knock at the door could be a letter of good news or bad, or even Jack himself returned. Week by week, Gert continued her enquiries, but each came back with a similar response that presumed he had been killed.

In January 1919, nearly six months after she had first heard Jack was missing, and over a year since she last saw him, Gert received the following letter. It is more definitive than those previously received, and hopefully gave some condolence.

I will now give you some information which has long been on my mind. Your husband was wounded in the knee. Well, after we had finished the raid, the Battalion came out for rest and were relieved by another Battalion. During my stay in hospital I ran across some of these fellows. While they were out on patrol, they came across a Sergeant Major dead in a shell hole and on enquiring as to his description I am sorry to say that he answered to the description of your husband and from the position they described it was just where I saw him sitting when he was wounded.

I assure you that it upsets me very much to tell you this but I felt it my duty to and it must be a big suspense on your mind, but I can assure you that your husband was a soldier and a gentleman and loved by all the boys who came under his command. He will be sadly missed by all of us.

---

13 Royal Armouries, ADAM A4/11, K. Robson, British Red Cross and Order of St. John, to Gert Adam, 19 November 1918.
14 Imperial War Museum, *History of the Post Office Rifles*.

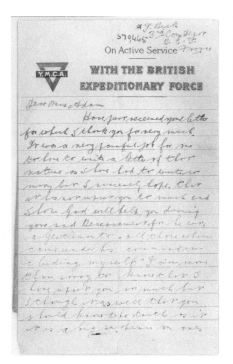
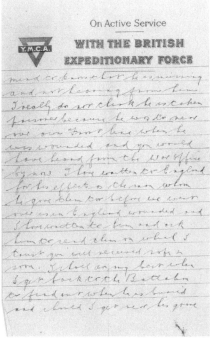

12 A letter from A.J. Bick to Gert about Jack, part of which reads 'he was an officer and a gentleman and loved by all the boys who came under his command'. © Royal Armouries. ADAM A4/18.

Trusting this letter will find you all well. May God help you bear the misfortune that has befallen you.

Yours sincerely,

A. J. Bick.[15]

'A Sergeant Major dead in a shell hole'. It was the news Gert had feared.

Not until 2 December 1919, more than a year after the official end of the war, did Gert receive a letter from the War Office. It stated that as Jack was missing since 25 July 1918 'and that, as no further information concerning him has since been received, it has been presumed for official purposes that he died on or since that date and is presumed dead'.[16] Jack's body was never found and Gert was widowed aged thirty-six with three young children.

In 1922, Gert received Jack's British War Medal, Victory Medal and commemorative plaque issued by the War Office. These were in the box of letters acquired by the Royal Armouries, all still in their postal envelopes, opened but not displayed. The collection also contained details of memorial services held in Doncaster, a photograph of the memorial in Pozieres cemetery in France where Jack's name was inscribed, and a letter about a Teacher's Memorial in London's County Hall unveiled in October 1924. It is not known if Gert

15 Royal Armouries, ADAM A4/18, A.J. Bick to Gert Adam, January 1919.
16 Royal Armouries, ADAM A4/5, War Office to Gert Adam, 2 December 1919.

No.E/784387/ (Accts. 4.)   Effects—Form 100c.

CERTIFIED that it appears from the records of this Office that

No. 388027 Company Sergeant Major John Gill Simpson Adams, 8th (City of London) Battalion, The London Regiment, was missing on the *twenty-fifth* day of *July 1918,* and that, as no further information concerning him has since been received, it has been presumed for official purposes that he died on or since that date.

The Soldier was serving on the above-mentioned date with the British Expeditionary Forces.

W E Brown

For the Assistant Financial Secretary.

Given at the War Office, London,

this *2nd* day of *December* 1919.

W4579—P3318 10,000 8/18 HWV(P15)   H18/7
1828—HP6108   5000   7/19

13 A War Office letter from December 1919 declaring that Jack was killed in action. © Royal Armouries. ADAM A4/5.

attended any memorial services. As Nicholson notes in her study of post-war life, although the war was over, 'formal occasions of remembrance designed to comfort often produced the reverse effect'.[17]

17 J. Nicholson, *The Great Silence 1918–1920: Living in the Shadow of the Great War* (London, 2009: John Murray), 5.

14 A mounted photograph of the memorial with Jack's name at Pozieres sent to Gert. © Royal Armouries. ADAM A5/6.

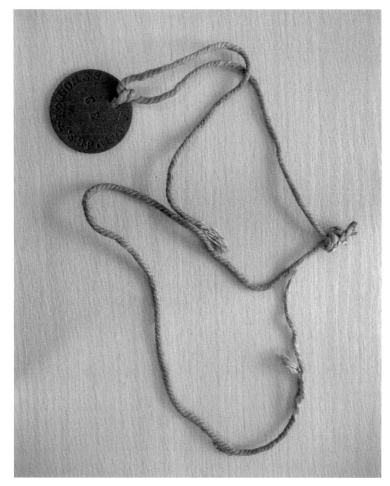

15 Jack's identity tags. Soldiers were issued with two sets of tags, one to wear and another to leave behind with one's belongings. © Royal Armouries. ADAM A1/5.

Within the collection the following two posthumous references about Jack were included, sent to Gert and kept by her.

> Mr J. G. S. Adam was well known to, and deeply respected by, a great number of London teachers. Previous to the war he was a member of the Committee of the London Teachers' Association, Secretary to the London Class Teachers' Association and a member of the Local Council (Finsbury and City) of the N.U.T. From this it is apparent Mr Adam was keenly interested in the affairs of his profession but this interest did not rest merely with professional associations. He loved children and loved a game. Consequently he was ever ready to work for anything which contributed to the happiness of the child. His association with the Islington and District School's Athletic Association and the North and East Islington Swimming Association was long and faithful, while for many years he was the life and soul of a football club of old boys of his school. He found times for many things because he had enthusiasm for them. Compounded as he was of sympathy, large heartedness, boundless energy and business

16 Jack's memorial plaque sent to Gert in 1920. © Royal Armouries. ADAM A1/12.

capacity, he will be long and kindly remembered by a large circle of his fellow teachers and old scholars.[18]

During his service at home he did invaluable work in the training of recruits. His untiring energy, combined with an ever-present sense of humour, kept his company always the most efficient in the Battalion, and his boys were not slow to appreciate him. He was always keen on their interests, whether in supervision of their meals, the organization of their sports, or taking the chair at their concerts. His devotion to all forms of sport persisted in army life and his company football team was always well to the front. In the sergeants mess he was always a keen critic of organisation and finance and a hard-working leader in social functions. His experience in teachers' organisations at home made him a very valuable asset to the whole battalion and in any re-shuffling of company commanders, there was always competition to get "Adam's Company". [19]

---

18 Royal Armouries, ADAM A4/30, reference by Mr J.J.C. Cooke about Jack Adam.
19 Royal Armouries, ADAM A4/31, reference by Mr Brown, Col. Sgt., 12th London Regiment, about Jack Adam.

CHAPTER FOUR

A CHANCE REUNION AND A NEW FIND

In 2006, Peter Spafford wrote a play entitled 'Only Water Between', based on the letters of Jack and Gert Adam and their three children. The story is interspersed with the memoirs of Hiram Maxim, inventor of the machine gun that wrought such havoc in the Great War. Maxim was born in 1840 and died in November 1916, before the full impact of his invention was realised. His memoirs speak of his intention to rid men from the battlefield by replacing them with the machine gun, but little thought was given to the countless thousands that the weapon could kill. The dichotomy of the tenderness in Jack and Gert's letters and the ambition of Hiram Maxim adds a chilling element to the tragedy of the story.

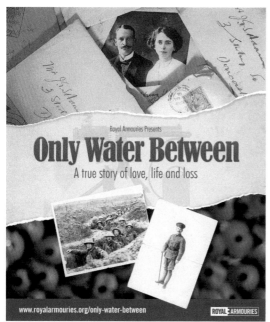

17 The poster for the play 'Only Water Between'.

The play was performed at the Royal Armouries Museum for the first time in 2006. It was well received by visitors, gaining interest from the local media, and was regularly performed at the museum. In 2008 the BBC recorded a short film with this book's editor about the collection, which was shown in Trafalgar Square as part of Remembrance Day, and the following year the play was taken to the Edinburgh Fringe Festival to reach a wider audience, where it was very well received. The play was performed again in 2014 as part of the centenary commemorations in the region.

One day, after a performance at the museum, a member of the audience had approached the cast and said that they recognised the names of those involved. Sure enough when they contacted their friends, it did transpire to be their grandparents' letters. Francis and Faith, the two children of Jack and Gert's daughter Peg, were still living in the area and were delighted to hear that the letters had been found. They had been accidentally lost in a house move some years before. Francis and Faith came to watch the play in Leeds and were able to fill in some gaps in the story as well as share what happened to the children. They also made the trip up to Edinburgh.

In February 2009 the rest of the story revealed itself. Whilst sorting out some of their parents' belongings Francis and Faith stumbled across a package wrapped in an old pink shawl. Opening it, they found a selection of letters, photographs and a leather wallet, and knew instantly whose they were. It transpired that Gert had selected her most personal letters from Jack and kept these apart from the rest; these had become separated and accidentally lost prior to the Royal Armouries acquiring the bulk of the letters in 2006. This additional collection of letters contained Jack's pocket diary from the front, mentioned in early letters to Gert, and more letters sent between the couple in June and July 1918 prior to Jack's disappearance.

Two letters in this new collection are particularly poignant. The first was written on 24 July 1918; it turned out to be Jack's last scribbled note to Gert and his 'little cubs'. Never actually posted, it fortunately managed to find its way to Gert along with his other belongings.

> To my darling and My little cubs. God bless you. We go over tomorrow and I may be unlucky. God bless you all. It's hard but, well I feel very cheery about it. I love you darling, I always have. My own, Brown Bear.[1]

The other letter was again unposted, and the envelope simply read: 'In case, G Adam'. It contains a letter written by Jack in February 1918 for his wife in case the worst was to happen. It is a long letter with lots of financial information and advice, but here is an edited account:

> Darling,
>
> It's somewhat difficult to imagine that one has gone under and write from the other side. Still in view of the possibility I ought to write something.
>
> I may say if I am knocked out I shall be surprised. The casualties among my rank are very few. Well as far as life is concerned I have no complaints to make. Except that I was not able to provide for you quite as I should have wished but the three children who caused the inconvenience will now repay for it. It would have been a great pity had I left no one behind to comfort you.
>
> For ourselves I have not a single regret or fault to find. You are darling exactly all that a woman should be and to me perfect. Would I had been so good as yourself. I love you if I may make myself equal to you but I more worship. You are more an object of worship than love. I think ours was a perfect match. I had the common sense of the average man and you the goodness

---

1 Royal Armouries, ADAM B2/18, Jack Adams to Gert Adams, unposted, found in wallet, dated 24 July 1918.

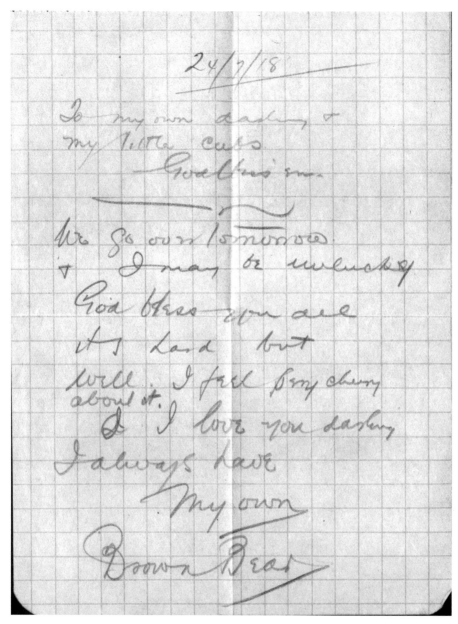

18 Jack's final note to his family written on 24 July 1918. © Royal Armouries. ADAM B2/18.

and love of the best little woman in the world. Greater things I believe were in store for us had I remained with you but when our country is in need I have no hesitation in making the final sacrifice. Much more I think darling but you can realise the difficulty of the expression. My love story has been equal to anyone in the world and leaves nothing to be desired.[2]

2 Royal Armouries, ADAM B2/4, Jack Adam to Gert Adam, dated 4 February 1918, carried on his person and returned to Gert after his death.

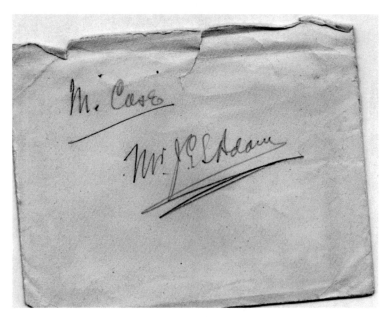

19 The envelope of Jack's 'In case of death' letter written 4 February 1918. © Royal Armouries. ADAM B2/4.

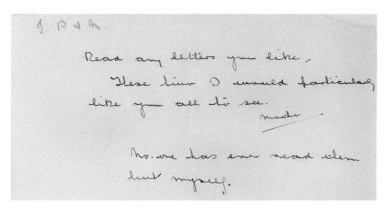

20 A note from Gert to the children, encouraging them to read the letters. © Royal Armouries. ADAM B4/18.

Whilst it had originally been unclear as to whether the three children ever saw the letters from their father, a note by Gert to the children in this second collection implies that they did:

> 'J. P & M. Read any letters you like. These five I would particularly like you all to see. Mother. No-one has ever read them but myself.'[3]

3 Royal Armouries, ADAM B4/18, note from Gert Adam in the second selection of letters found in 2009.

These letters also had a further selection of photographs and postcards showing Jack with various regiments and also images of the children and Gert, which he must have carried with him. Francis and Faith generously decided to donate these new-found letters and photographs to the Royal Armouries Museum so that they could be kept with the rest of their family's collection and preserved for the future.

With the decision in 1915 that no corpses would be returned home, along with the sheer number of those who were unidentifiable and not found, the lack of evidence of death gave rise in many, an inability to believe in death. The couple's grandchildren informed us that Gert continued to write letters asking for information about Jack. Her passport, issued on 27 July 1937, showed two visits to France: Dieppe from 2 August to 14 August 1937, and Saint Malo, Normandy from 14 August to 20 August 1938.[4] One might assume they had been to visit memorials and sites her husband had been, but Jack Junior later told his family that he accompanied his mother as she visited hospitals, still in the hope of finding her husband nearly twenty years on. She never gave up hope that he might still be alive, and never re-married.

In his 'in case of death' letter, Jack advised Gert that 'financially you should be sound to the end'.[5] For many war widows the 'pensions were always miserly',[6] and depended on variables such as the rank of the deceased, the age of the widow and the number of children. Often the amount paid was simply not enough, and the women had to return to work or take up new employment. Pensions were not a statutory right and women were also at the mercy of others' judgement to receive them. It was noted that children in work increased considerably during and after the war, again revealing the shortfall faced by families with husbands and fathers overseas – even more so if they were killed.[7] Gert was one of the lucky ones. Because of Jack's rank as a Company Sergeant Major, she would have received at least three times that of a private soldier's widow. This was supplemented by his teacher's pension. She was also living with her parents, which may have reduced her worries about rent or accommodation. They would also have been vital support for her. Jack had written in his 'in case of death' letter:

'To your mother please give my thanks for the thousand and one ways in which she has helped me. She works too hard – much too hard. I wish I could have seen her having a well-deserved rest, I loved her almost as well as my own. God grant that you may have her many years to comfort you.'[8]

Although there was no happy ending for Jack and Gert, their three children went on to be very successful. Jack had left the following advice for Gert in his 'in case of death' letter:

The kiddies are excellent in health and provided you are strict will be a great comfort to you. Now is the time to be strict with them and in your place, I should be almost unfair. The goodness cannot keep oozing from yourself and in endeavouring to be fair to them you will love not wisely but too well. Particularly Jackie. The girls I think you will manage well but the boy may outstrip you. Now I should have instant obedience from him in small things. Don't pamper him let him fight his way out. One has no respect for people who allow you to do as you like. I think he has brains and your great difficulty will be to get him to join in physical exercises.

4 Royal Armouries, ADAM A6/1, passport of Gert Adam, issued 27 July 1937.
5 Royal Armouries, ADAM B2/4, Jack Adam to Gert Adam, 4 February 1918.
6 Van Emden, *The Quick and the Dead*, 214.
7 Van Emden, *The Quick and the Dead*, 217–226.
8 Royal Armouries, ADAM B2/4, Jack Adam to Gert Adam, dated 4 February 1918.

21 Images of the children and a faded print of Gert, possibly carried by Jack in his wallet. ADAM B4/7A, B4/7B, B4/15.

22 Undated photograph of Jack Adam in uniform (standing) alongside J. Gardner. © Royal Armouries. ADAM A5/3.

Encourage sport of all kinds. A good sportsman can't be a bad man. The lack of concentration (inherited from myself) will stop him being the success which his brains would take him to, but you should assist him in this by perfect order in the minutest detail at home. In his early reading see that he knows what he has read and whatever job he has on hand see it is carried out to the end. I would have like him to be a doctor or lawyer he has (or should have from my father and myself) the logical mind suited to a solicitor and it may be possible to get him on to the right road for that. If this is too much, then a teacher would suit him. And in this J. Gardner or Ed Wolstenholme or L F Brown would assist you, and you must not forget to get their assistance. In my short time in London I did a great deal for the profession and they will be pleased to assist. The girls I leave to you and hope they will be like their mother I am afraid they will have a job.[9]

9 Royal Armouries, ADAM B2/4, Jack Adam to Gert Adam, dated 4 February 1918.

There were other mentions of J. Gardner in Jack's letters. The grandchildren knew him well and informed us that he had been part of Jack's children's lives; the two men had obviously agreed that should the worse happen, they would look out for each other's families.

Despite losing their father, Gert's strength empowered her children to do well. Jack had advised her to keep a firm hand with Jack junior and his concerns for his son echoed throughout his letters: 'So Jack couldn't get a job as a cattle driver. I wish I had been there; I would have got one for him. Never mind. I'll look after him one day.'[10] He need not have worried though. Jack achieved a first from the University of Oxford and became canon of Blackburn Cathedral. Peggy married Donald Hewitt, a curate at Balby Church who later became Canon and Vicar Choral of York Minster. Their son Francis followed suit.

Madge, the baby of the family, was awarded a scholarship to Doncaster High School, and later to Oxford, where she became the first woman to get a first in physics at St Hugh's College. After completing a doctorate at Lady Margaret Hall, Madge became a solar astronomer, internationally renowned for her work on sunspots and their magnetic fields, and was later elected a Fellow of the Royal Astronomical Society.[11]

10 Royal Armouries, ADAM A2/64, Jack Adam to Gert Adam, 23 June 1918.

11 K. Williams, 'Madge Adam: solar physicist acclaimed for her work on sunspots and magnetic fields', *Guardian*, 10 September 2001; C.M.C. Haines, *International Women in Science: A Biographical Dictionary to 1950* (Santa Barbara, California, 2001: ABC-CLIO), 2; in addition to information provided by the family.

POSTSCRIPT

The impact of Jack's death on Gert, his family, friends and three young children can only be imagined. The correspondence between the couple serves as a reminder of the impact of the First World War on the lives of so many individuals and families throughout the country, and sheds fresh light on the circumstances of the wives and children left behind. Whilst their lives may not have been directly involved in the war or war work, they would be forever altered. In some ways Gert and Jack's story is one of the more fortunate ones. Their separation, although permanent, came only during the last year of the war, and Jack went willingly as a volunteer. His rank ensured that Gert received a good separation allowance – and, later, a good widow's allowance – and she was able to reside with family without needing to work. But the most poignant memory of this family's story is the anxious wait for news and the impact on family life caused by separation and in this case, the loss of a husband and father.

GV RI

Dieu et mon Droit

HE whom this scroll commemorates was numbered among those who, at the call of King and Country, left all that was dear to them, endured hardness, faced danger, and finally passed out of the sight of men by the path of duty and self-sacrifice, giving up their own lives that others might live in freedom. Let those who come after see to it that his name be not forgotten.

Coy. Serjt. Maj. John Gill Simpson Adam London Regt.

23 The certificate of thanks sent to Gert. © Royal Armouries. ADAM A1/14.

SELECT BIBLIOGRAPHY

I. Beckett, *Home Front 1914–1918: How Britain Survived the Great War* (London, 2006: The National Archives)

A. Clare, 'A personal account of the Home Front', in M. Andrews and J. Lomas (eds.), *The Home Front in Britain: Images, Myths and Forgotten Experiences since 1914* (London, 2014: Palgrave Macmillan)

A. Clare, *For King and Country: Calderdale's First World War Centenary 2014–2018* (Halifax, 2015: Calderdale Museums)

R. van Emden, *The Quick and the Dead: Fallen Soldiers and Their Families in the Great War* (London, 2011: Bloomsbury)

P. Fussell, *The Great War and Modern Memory* (Oxford, 1975: Oxford University Press)

S. Humphries and R. van Emden, *All Quiet on the Home Front: An Oral History of Life in Britain During the First World War* (London, 2004: Headline Publishing Group)

Imperial War Museum, *History of the Post Office Rifles, 8th Battalion City of London Regiment 1914–1918* (London, 1997: Imperial War Museum)

J. Nicholson, *The Great Silence 1918–1920: Living in the Shadow of the Great War* (London, 2009: John Murray)

M. Roper, *The Secret Battle: Emotional Survival in the Great War* (Manchester, 2010: Manchester University Press)